How to Let Go of Self-Doubt, Embrace Your Unique Beauty, and Create a Life Filled with Joy and Confidence

Infinite Echo Publishing

THIS JOURNAL BELONGS TO

NAME

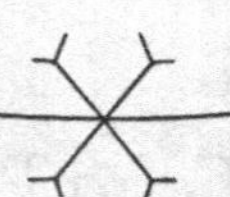

Table of Contents

Table of Contents

Introduction

Welcome to the *Self-Love Journal for Black Teen Girls*—a warm, welcoming space created just for you. In these pages, you'll explore what it means to embrace your identity, celebrate your beauty, and nurture the power within you. As you reflect on your daily experiences, dreams, and challenges, remember that your story is unique and worthy of being told. This journal will guide you toward greater self-awareness, resilience, and confidence, reminding you every day that you are radiant, you are strong, and most importantly—you are loved. Let's begin this journey together, one page at a time.

What Does It Mean to Love Yourself?

Self-love is treating yourself like you matter—because you do. It's looking in the mirror, seeing your hair, your skin, and your features, and knowing you are beautiful just as you are. It's cutting out the negative noise that tries to tell you otherwise. Deep down, you deserve the best from the people around you—and from yourself.

Think about that moment when you feel unstoppable—like you can walk into your classroom or onto a stage and let your brilliance shine. That's your confidence taking the lead.

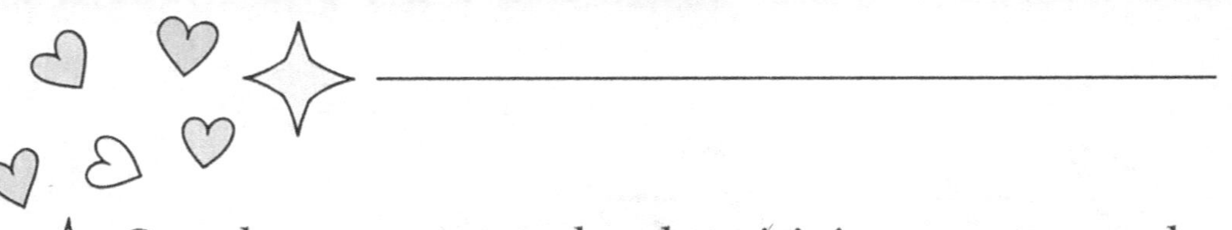

Or when someone hurls criticism your way, but it doesn't stick, because you know who you are and what you're worth. That's your self-esteem at work. And when you decide not to give time or energy to folks who don't respect you, that's you owning your self-worth.

Cultivating these qualities isn't always easy, especially in a world that sometimes overlooks or underestimates Black girls. But every single day, you have the power to remind yourself of your value. Maybe that means cherishing the beauty of your hair in every style it takes—curly, braided, natural, or otherwise—and owning the brilliance you bring wherever you go. With each small act of kindness toward yourself—each compliment, each boundary you set, each goal you reach—you're showing you love who you are, inside and out.

Remember: you are powerful, intelligent, and worthy. And every time you honor that truth, you're practicing self-love.

How to Use This Book

This book is your personal space to nurture self-love and confidence, every single day. Think of it as a conversation with yourself—one that honors your identity as a Black teen girl and celebrates the strength and beauty you already have inside.

Each day, you'll find simple questions to help you reflect on how you're feeling and how you can uplift yourself.

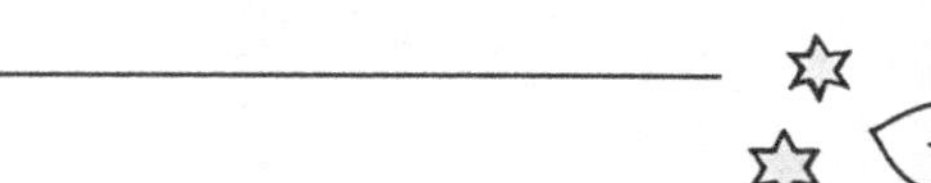

For example:

- What is one small act of kindness I can do for myself today?
- When I look in the mirror, what do I notice that is beautiful about me (inside or out)?
- I am grateful for...

These questions remind you that self-love isn't just a big, dramatic event—it's also the small moments of care you show yourself. Write down your answers in this journal, and watch how these positive habits brighten your mindset over time.

On certain days, you'll dive deeper with bigger, one-time questions.

These might look like:

- What does self-love mean to me, and why is it important?
- How have I grown or changed for the better over the past year?
- Who in my life inspires me to be my best self, and why?

These prompts allow you to explore your hopes, dreams, and the influences that shape who you are. By taking the time to really think about these, you'll uncover new insights about yourself—and celebrate your growth along the way.

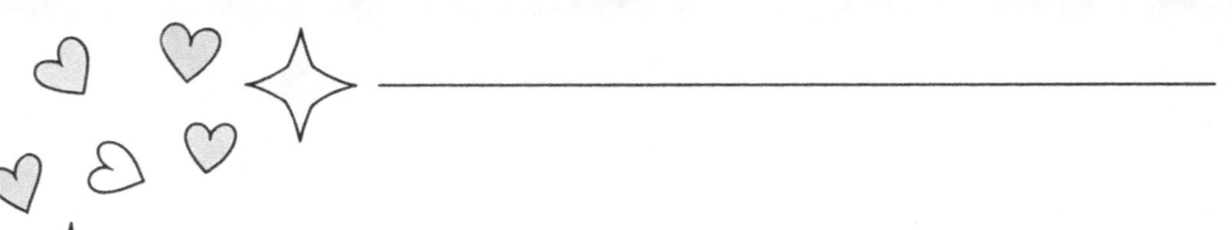
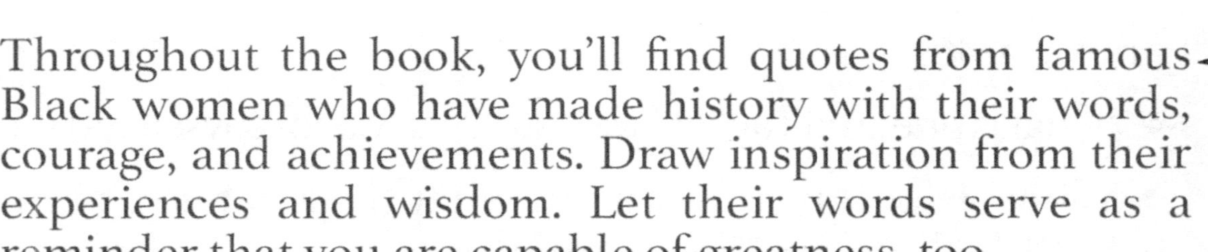

Throughout the book, you'll find quotes from famous Black women who have made history with their words, courage, and achievements. Draw inspiration from their experiences and wisdom. Let their words serve as a reminder that you are capable of greatness, too

This journal is for you, so feel free to add your own flair. You can jot down extra thoughts, sketch or doodle how you feel, write out your favorite song lyrics, or even tuck in affirmations on sticky notes. The goal is to fill these pages with your truth—because everything that makes you "you" is worth celebrating

Try setting aside a few minutes each day—maybe right after school or before bed—to write in your journal. If you skip a day, don't worry. Show yourself kindness and hop back in when you can. Over time, you'll notice a stronger sense of self-confidence and peace within you.

As you answer these prompts, you're also creating a record of how far you've come. Look back at your early entries now and then. You'll see how your answers evolve, reflecting your growth, resilience, and deeper self-love. Be proud of that!

This book is here to remind you that you are powerful, worthy, and enough—every single day. Let it serve as your safe space to explore, honor, and cherish who you are, both inside and out. And remember: your words have power, so use them to uplift yourself as you continue to shine.

Day 1

What is one small act of kindness I can do for myself today?

When I look in the mirror, what do I notice that is beautiful about me (inside or out)?

I am grateful for...

1.

2.

3.

What does self-love mean to me, and why is it important?

Day 2

What do I appreciate most about my personality today?

What's one small achievement from the past 24 hours that I can acknowledge and feel proud of?

I am grateful for...

1.

2.

3.

"Never be limited by other people's limited imaginations"
Dr. Mae Jemison

Day 3

What is one compliment I can give myself right now, without hesitation?

What negative thought about myself do I need to rewrite into something more loving or supportive?

I am grateful for...

1.

2.

3.

"Every great dream
begins with a
dreamer"
Harriet
Tubman
13

Day 4

What is one small act of kindness I can do for myself today?

When I look in the mirror, what do I notice that is beautiful about me (inside or out)?

I am grateful for...

1.

2.

3.

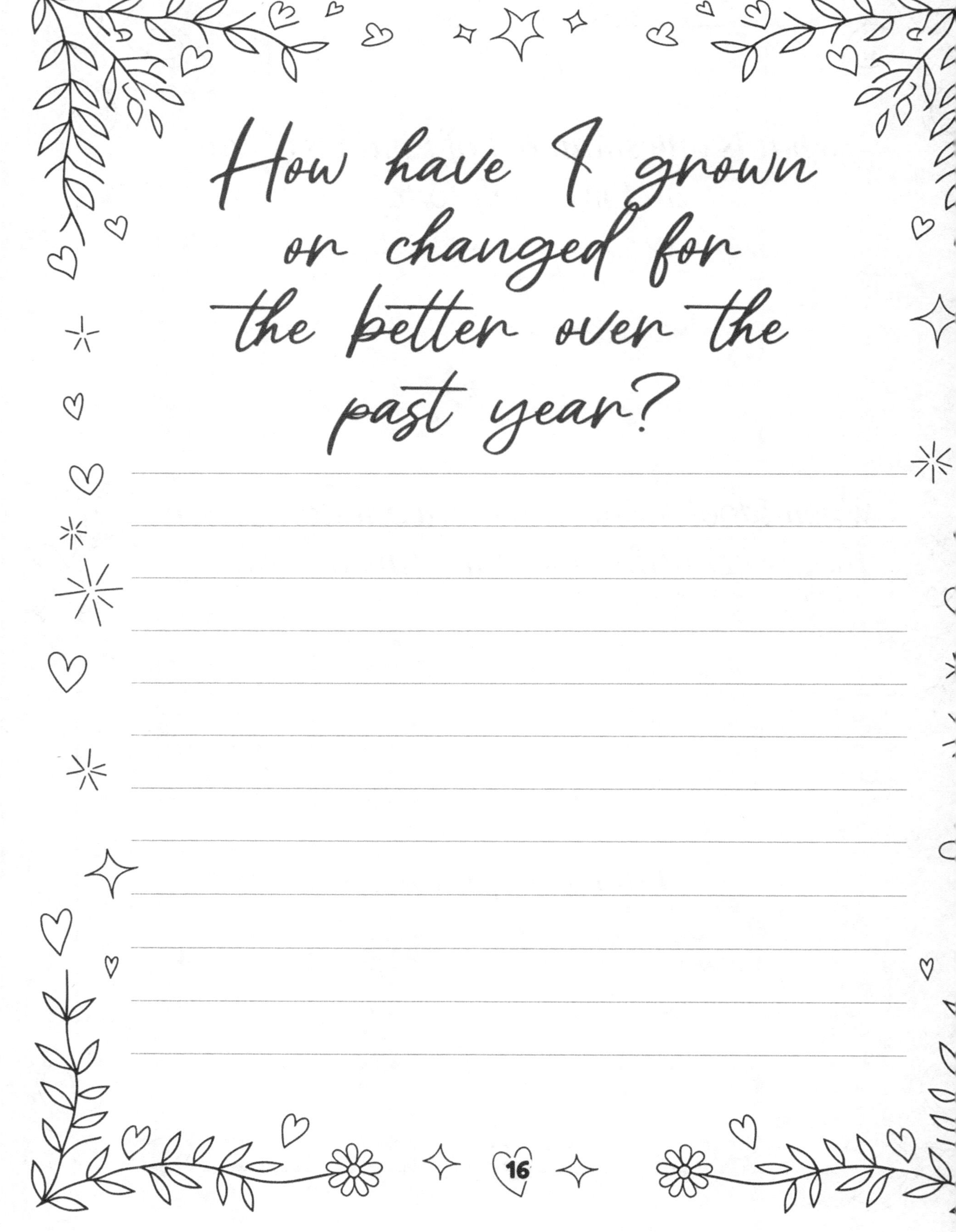

How have I grown or changed for the better over the past year?

Day 5

What do I appreciate most about my personality today?

What's one small achievement from the past 24 hours that I can acknowledge and feel proud of?

I am grateful for...

1.
2.
3.

"You can't be what you can't see"

Marian Wright Edelman

Day 6

What is one compliment I can give myself right now, without hesitation?

What negative thought about myself do I need to rewrite into something more loving or supportive?

I am grateful for...

1.

2.

3.

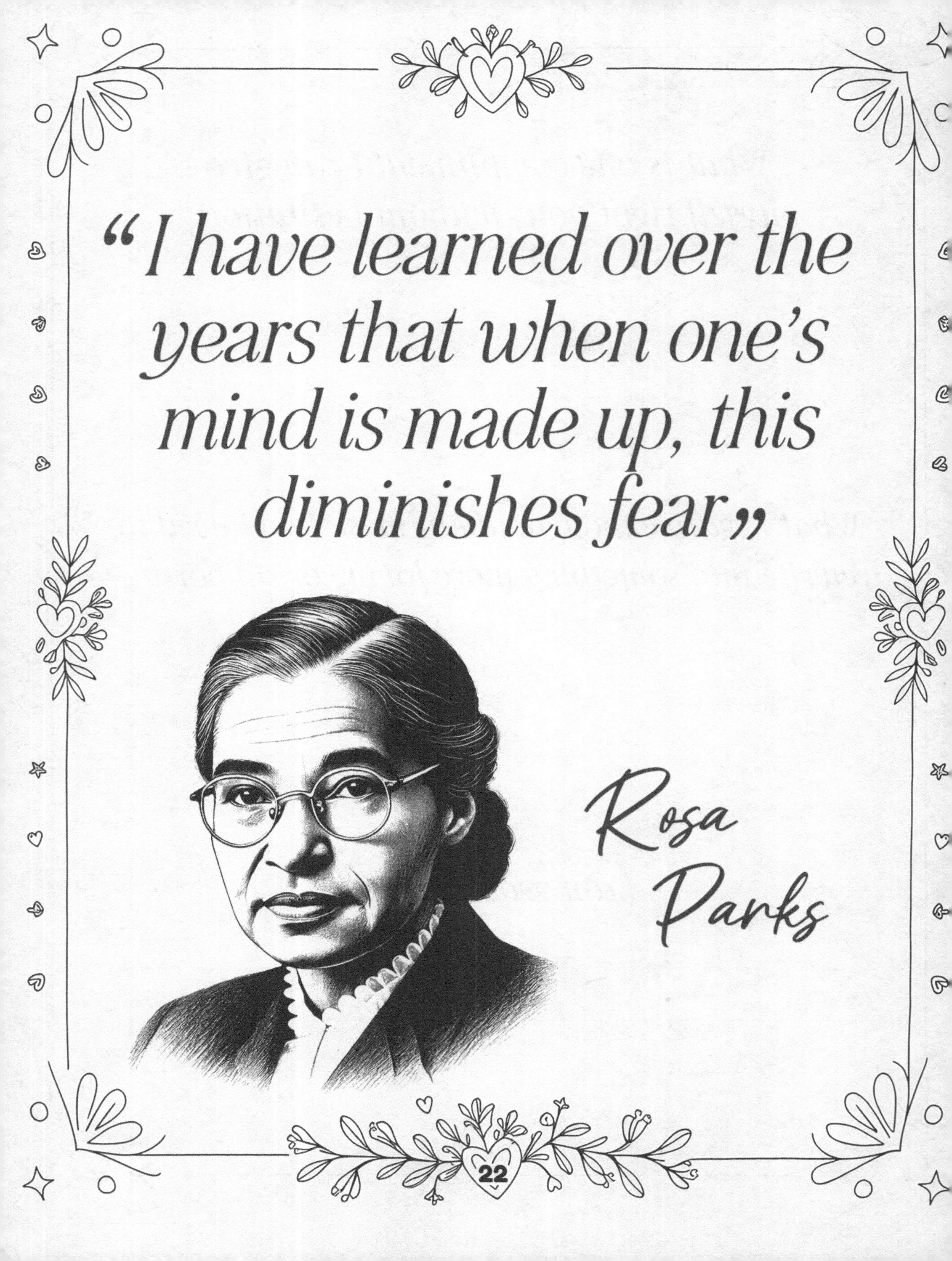
"I have learned over the years that when one's mind is made up, this diminishes fear"
Rosa Parks

Day 7

What is one small act of kindness I can do for myself today?

When I look in the mirror, what do I notice that is beautiful about me (inside or out)?

I am grateful for...

1.

2.

3.

Who in my life inspires me to be my best self, and why?

Day 8

What do I appreciate most about my personality today?

What's one small achievement from the past 24 hours that I can acknowledge and feel proud of?

I am grateful for...

1.

2.

3.

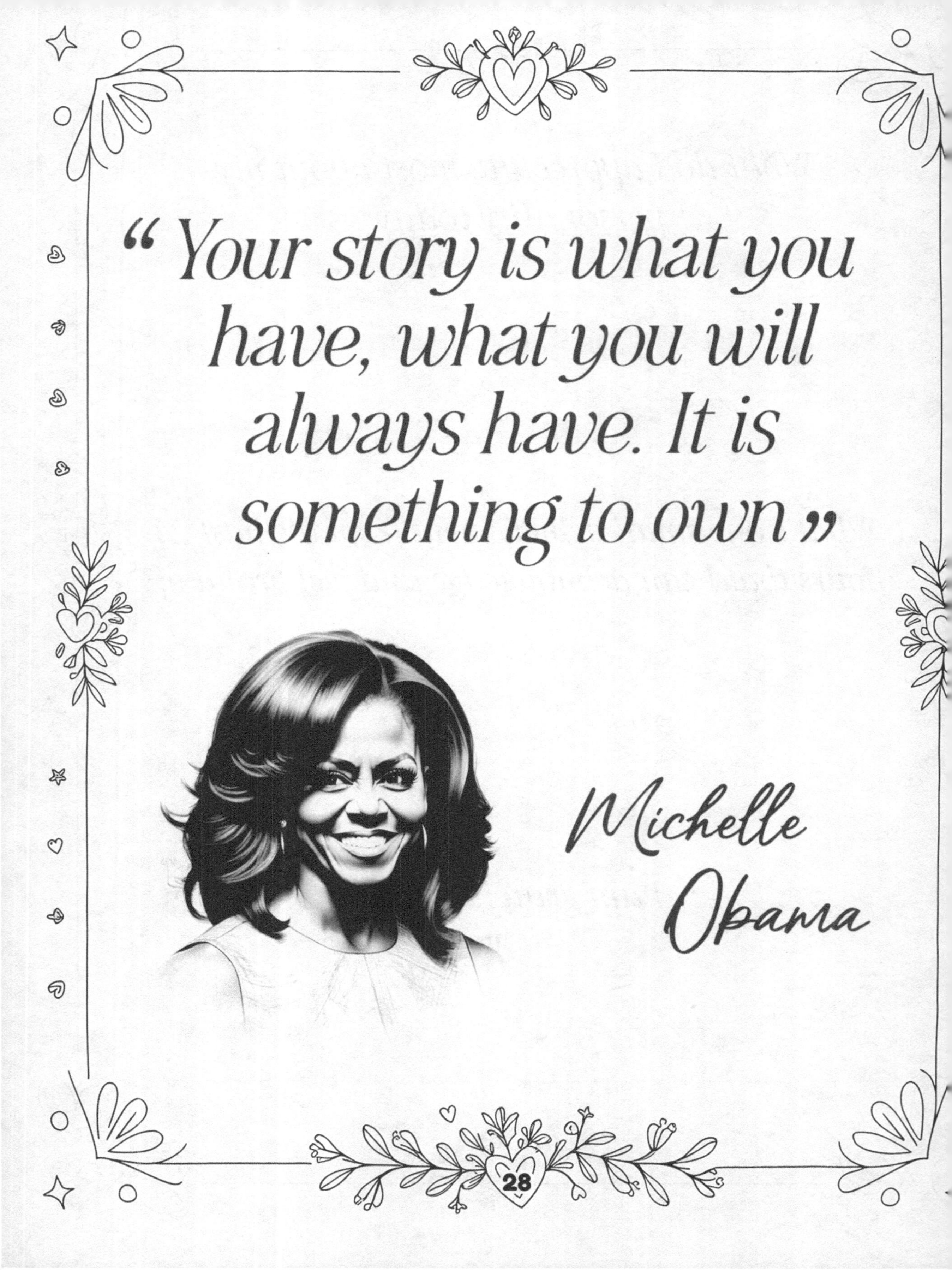

"Your story is what you have, what you will always have. It is something to own"

Michelle Obama

Day 9

What is one compliment I can give myself right now, without hesitation?

What negative thought about myself do I need to rewrite into something more loving or supportive?

I am grateful for...

1.

2.

3.

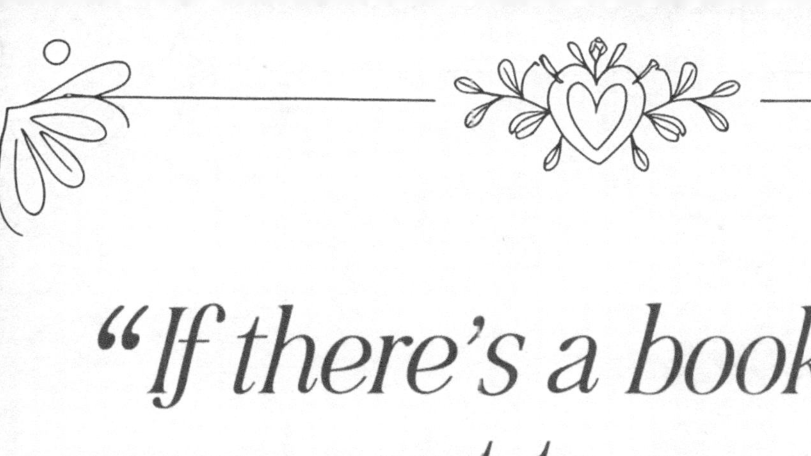

“If there’s a book that you want to read, but it hasn’t been written yet, then you must write it”

Toni Morrison

Day
10

What is one small act of kindness I can do for myself today?

When I look in the mirror, what do I notice that is beautiful about me (inside or out)?

I am grateful for...

1.

2.

3.

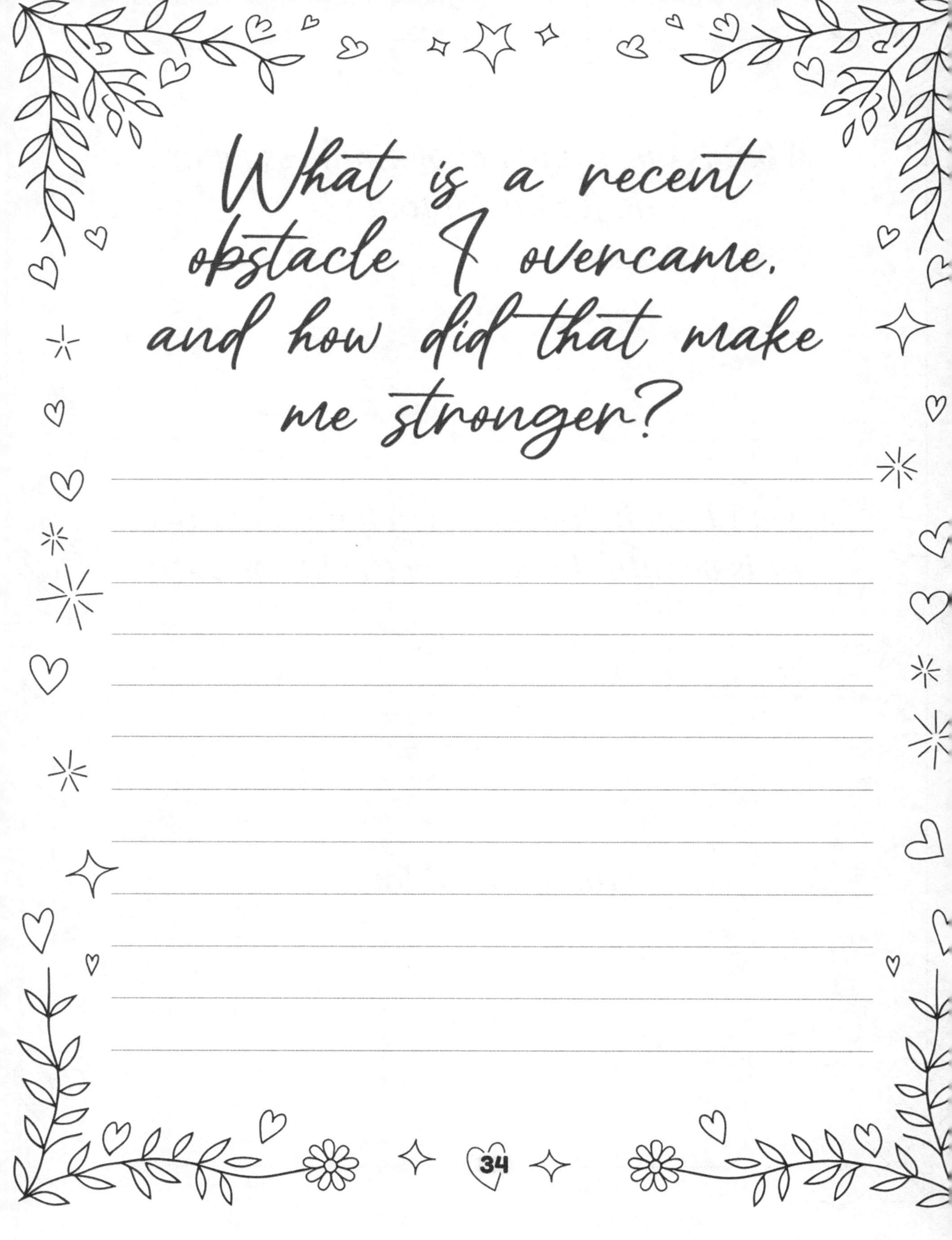

What is a recent obstacle I overcame, and how did that make me stronger?

Day 11

What do I appreciate most about my personality today?

What's one small achievement from the past 24 hours that I can acknowledge and feel proud of?

I am grateful for...

1.

2.

3.

"Caring for myself is not self-indulgence, it is self-preservation, and that is an act of political warfare"

Audre Lorde

Day 12

What is one compliment I can give myself right now, without hesitation?

What negative thought about myself do I need to rewrite into something more loving or supportive?

I am grateful for...

1.

2.

3.

“We all require and want respect, man or woman, Black or white. It’s our basic human right”
Aretha Franklin

Day 13

What is one small act of kindness I can do for myself today?

When I look in the mirror, what do I notice that is beautiful about me (inside or out)?

I am grateful for...

1.

2.

3.

What is one goal I'd like to accomplish this week, and why is it important to me?

Day 14

What do I appreciate most about my personality today?

What's one small achievement from the past 24 hours that I can acknowledge and feel proud of?

I am grateful for...

1.

2.

3.

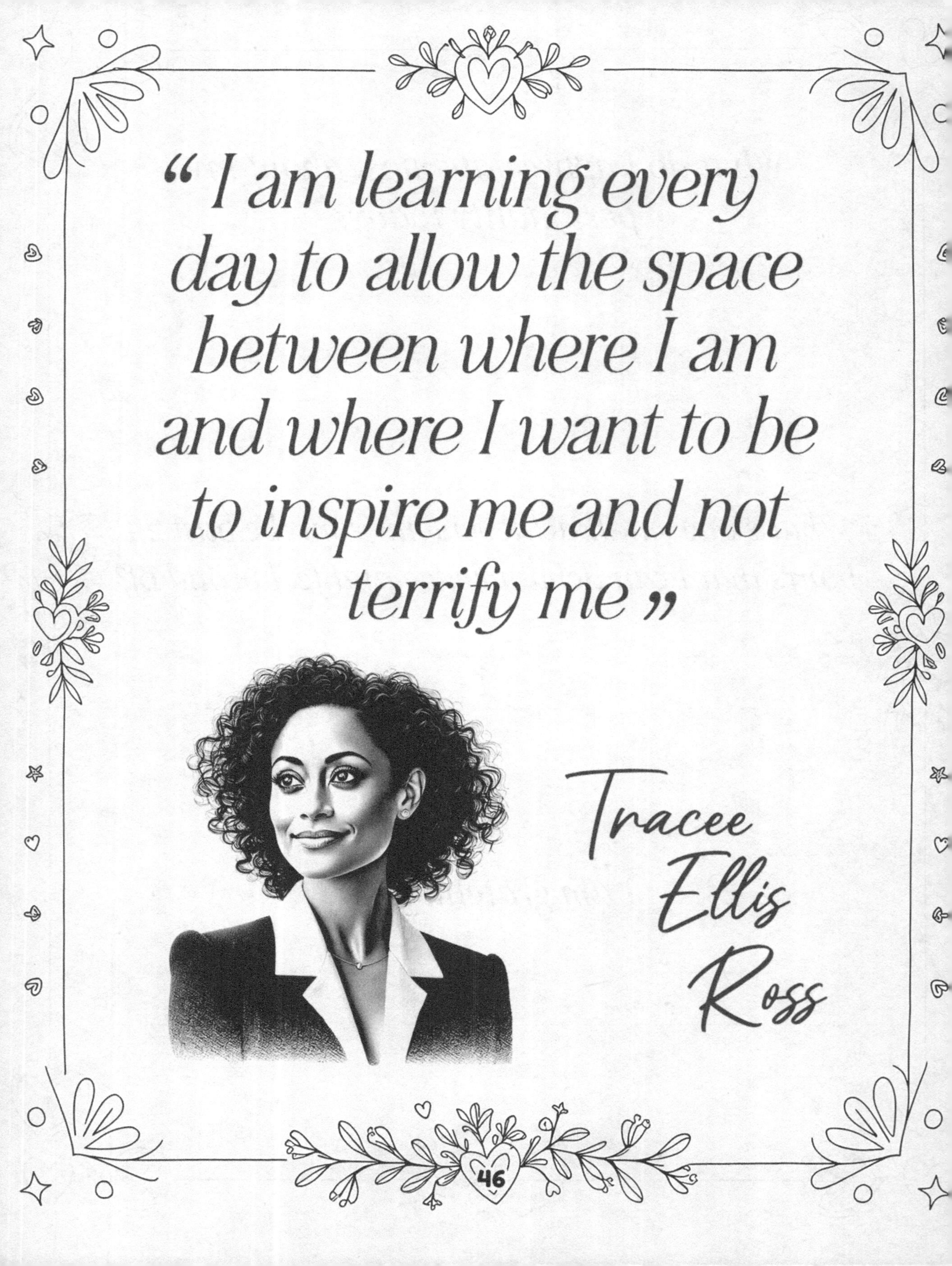

"I am learning every day to allow the space between where I am and where I want to be to inspire me and not terrify me"

Tracee Ellis Ross

Day 15

What is one compliment I can give myself right now, without hesitation?

What negative thought about myself do I need to rewrite into something more loving or supportive?

I am grateful for...

1.

2.

3.

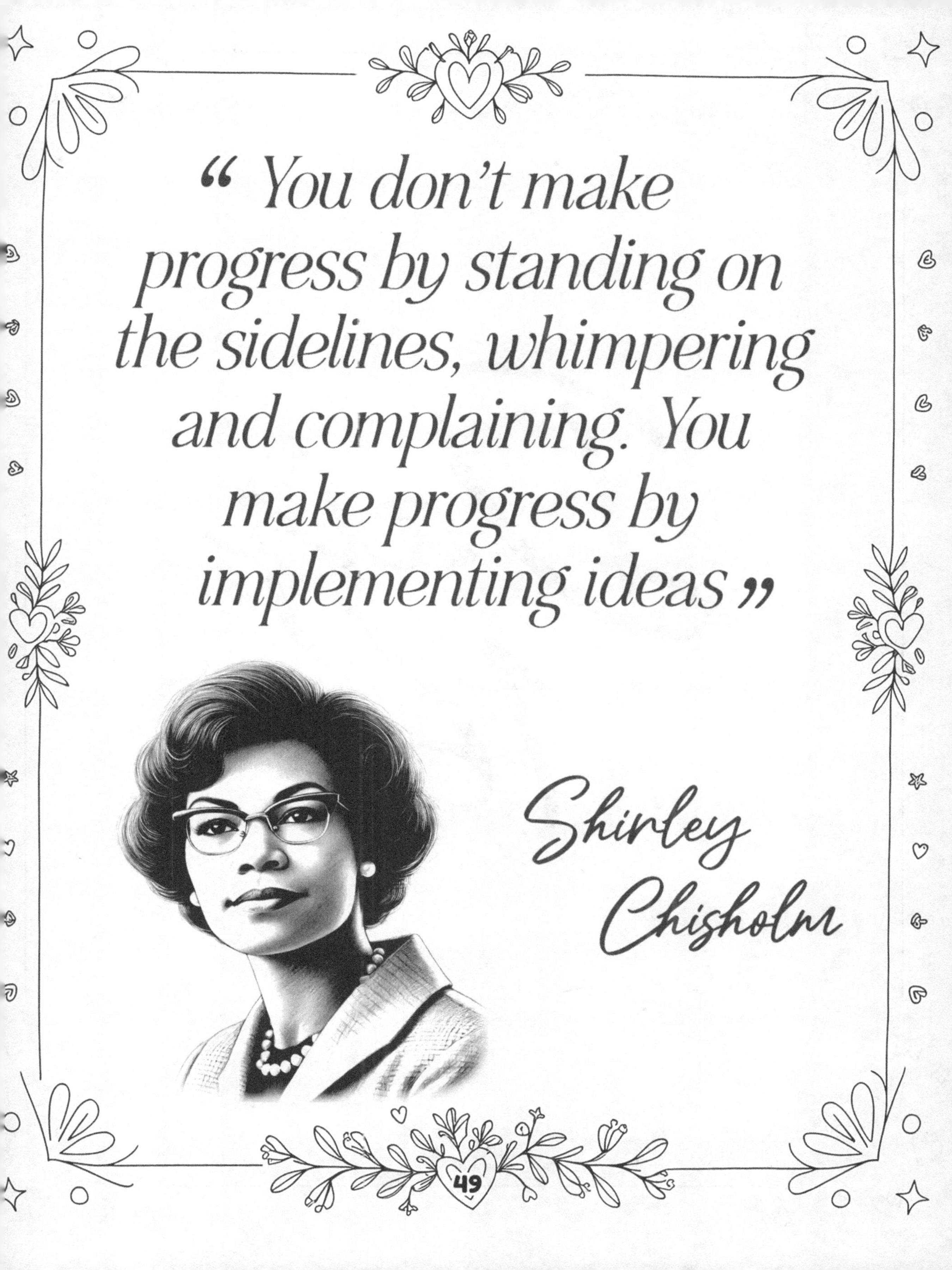
"You don't make
progress by standing on
the sidelines, whimpering
and complaining. You
make progress by
implementing ideas"
Shirley
Chisholm

Day
16

What is one small act of kindness I can do for myself today?

When I look in the mirror, what do I notice that is beautiful about me (inside or out)?

I am grateful for...

1.

2.

3.

Who is a Black woman I look up to, and what qualities of hers do I admire?

Day
17

What do I appreciate most about my personality today?

What's one small achievement from the past 24 hours that I can acknowledge and feel proud of?

I am grateful for...

1.
2.
3.

"I'm rooting for everybody Black"

Issa Rae

Day 18

What is one compliment I can give myself right now, without hesitation?

What negative thought about myself do I need to rewrite into something more loving or supportive?

I am grateful for...

1.
2.
3.

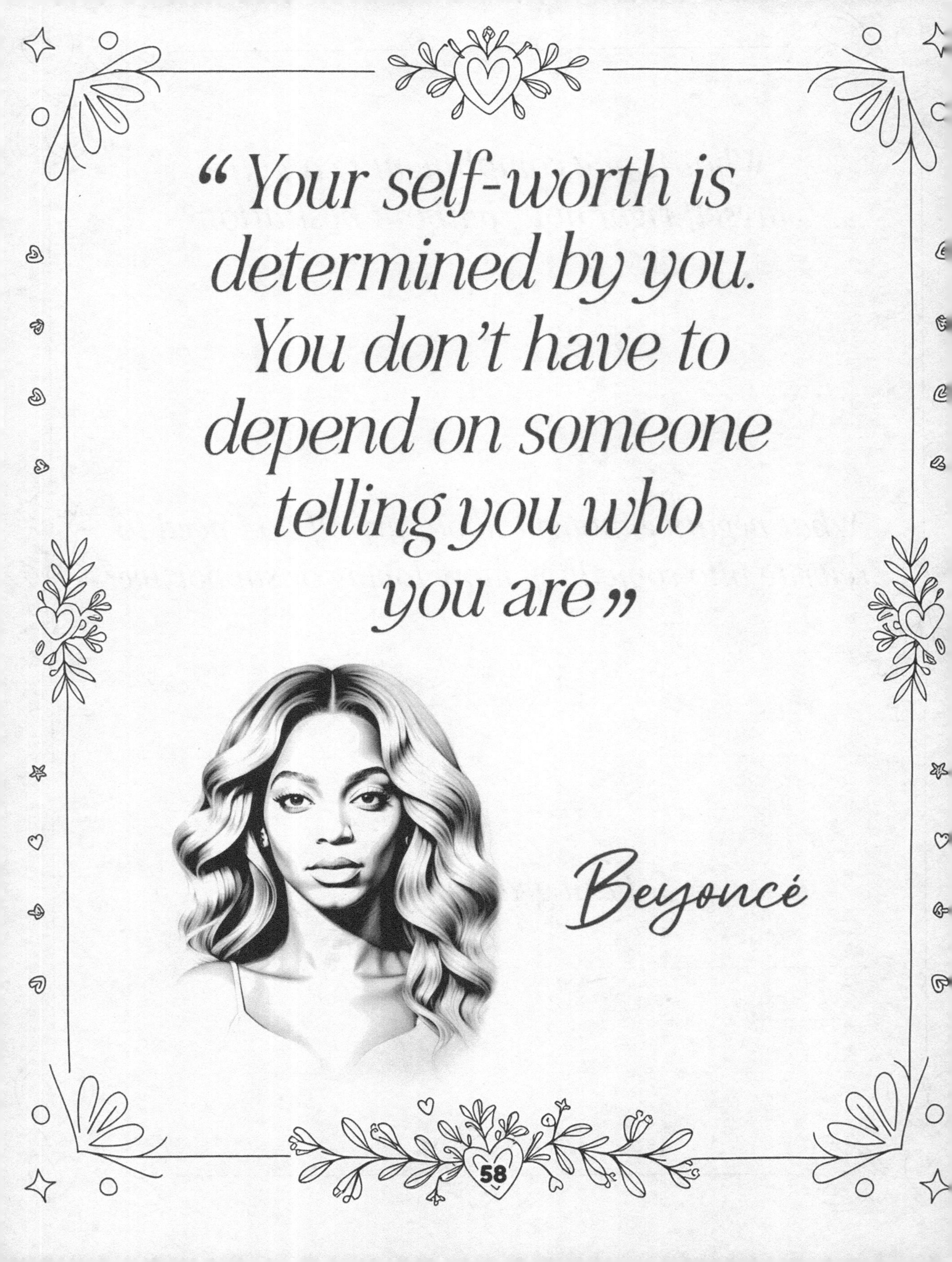

“Your self-worth is determined by you. You don’t have to depend on someone telling you who you are”

Beyoncé

Day
19

What is one small act of kindness I can do for myself today?

When I look in the mirror, what do I notice that is beautiful about me (inside or out)?

I am grateful for...

1.

2.

3.

How can I connect with my family or community today in a meaningful way?

Day
20

What do I appreciate most about my personality today?

What's one small achievement from the past 24 hours that I can acknowledge and feel proud of?

I am grateful for...

1.

2.

3.

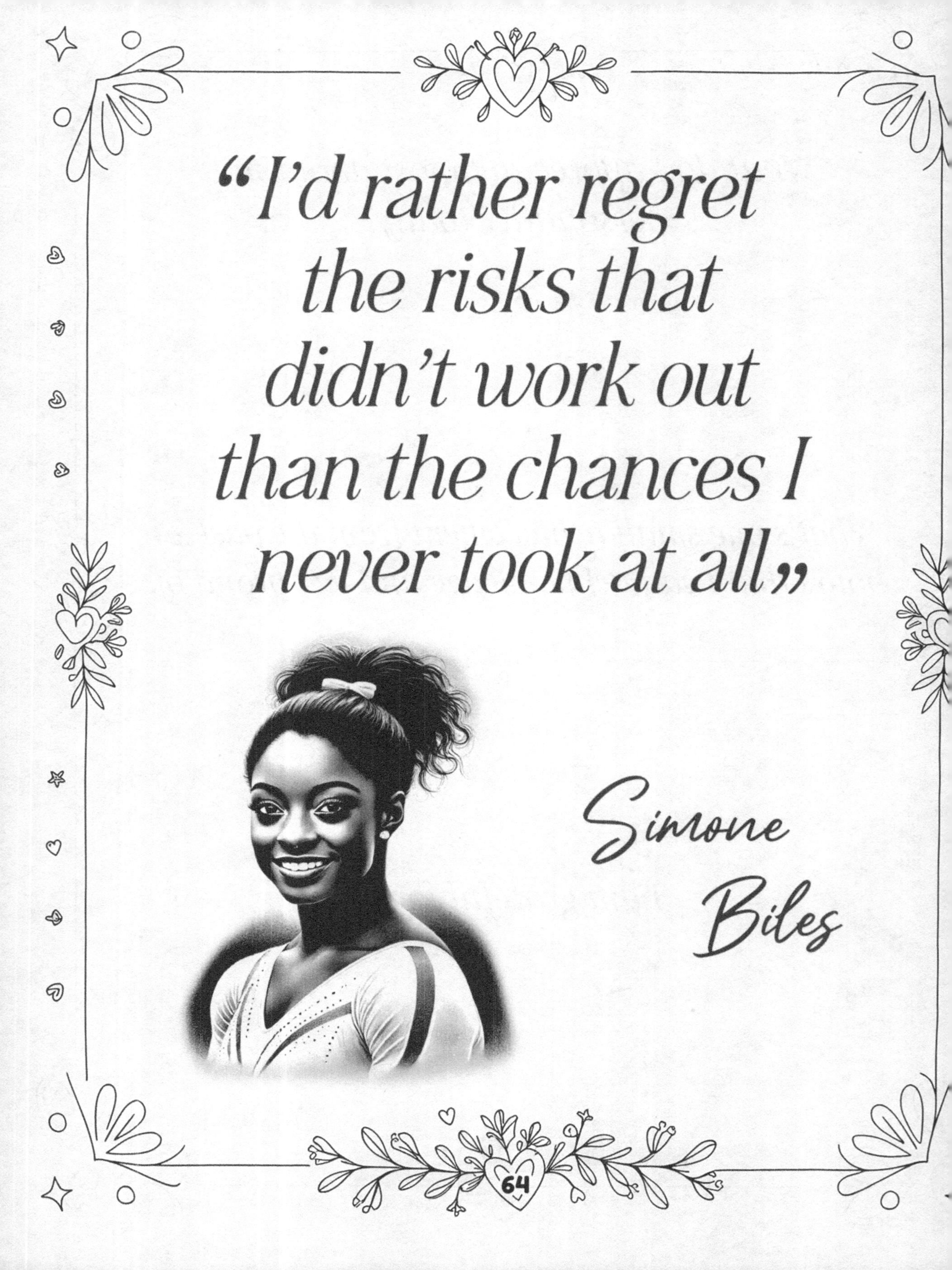
"I'd rather regret
the risks that
didn't work out
than the chances I
never took at all"
Simone
Biles

Day 21

What is one compliment I can give myself right now, without hesitation?

What negative thought about myself do I need to rewrite into something more loving or supportive?

I am grateful for...

1.

2.

3.

"There are so many great things in life; why dwell on negativity?"
Zendaya

Day
22

What is one small act of kindness I can do for myself today?

When I look in the mirror, what do I notice that is beautiful about me (inside or out)?

I am grateful for...

1.

2.

3.

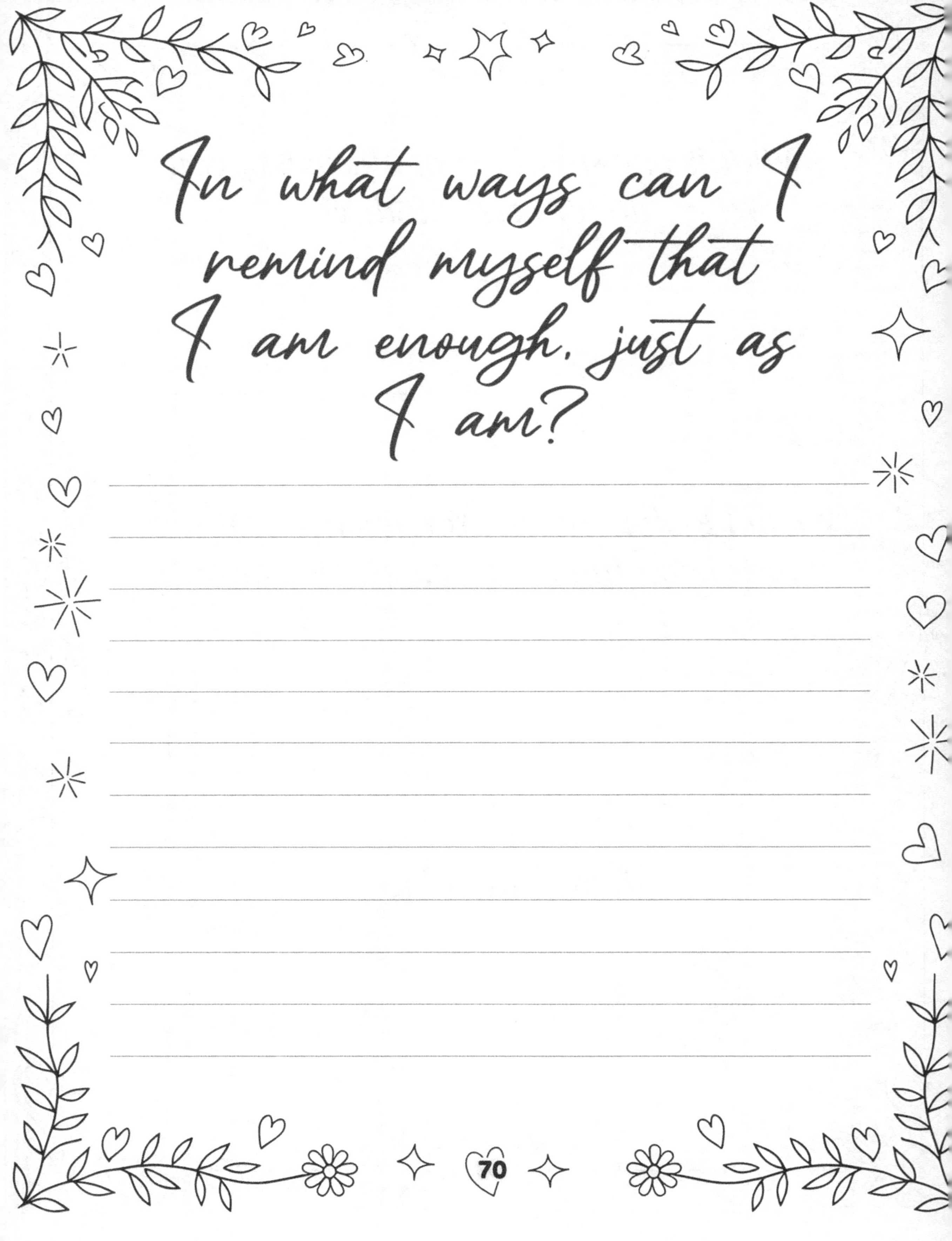

In what ways can I remind myself that I am enough, just as I am?

Day
23

What do I appreciate most about my personality today?

What's one small achievement from the past 24 hours that I can acknowledge and feel proud of?

I am grateful for...

1.

2.

3.

"What is
fundamentally
beautiful is compassion
for yourself and for
those around you"
Lupita
Nyong'o
73

Day 24

What is one compliment I can give myself right now, without hesitation?

What negative thought about myself do I need to rewrite into something more loving or supportive?

I am grateful for...

1.

2.

3.

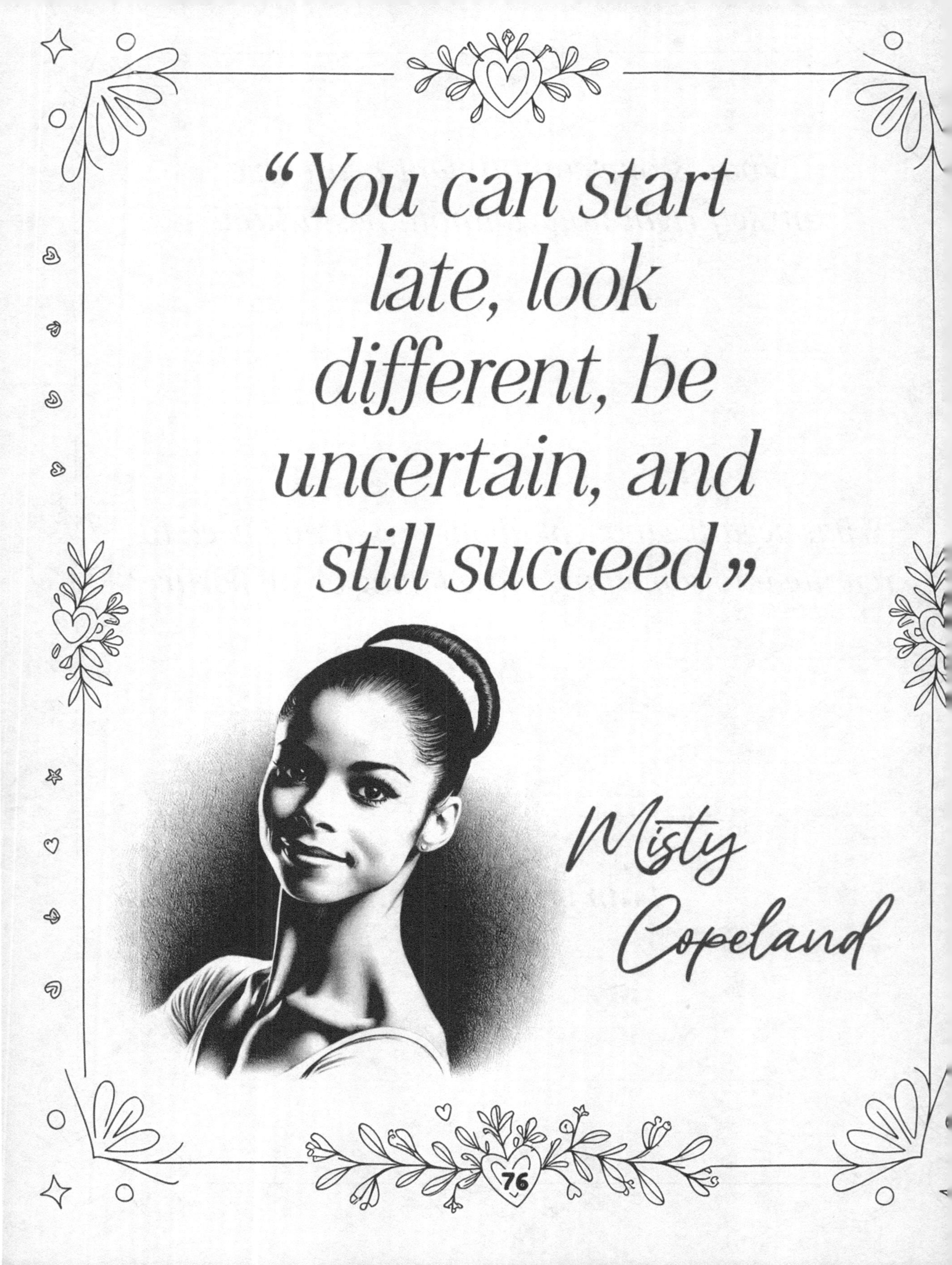
"You can start
late, look
different, be
uncertain, and
still succeed"
Misty
Copeland

Day
25

What is one small act of kindness I can do for myself today?

When I look in the mirror, what do I notice that is beautiful about me (inside or out)?

I am grateful for...

1.

2.

3.

What moment of joy or laughter did I experience recently, and how did it make me feel?

Day
26

What do I appreciate most about my personality today?

What's one small achievement from the past 24 hours that I can acknowledge and feel proud of?

I am grateful for...

1.

2.

3.

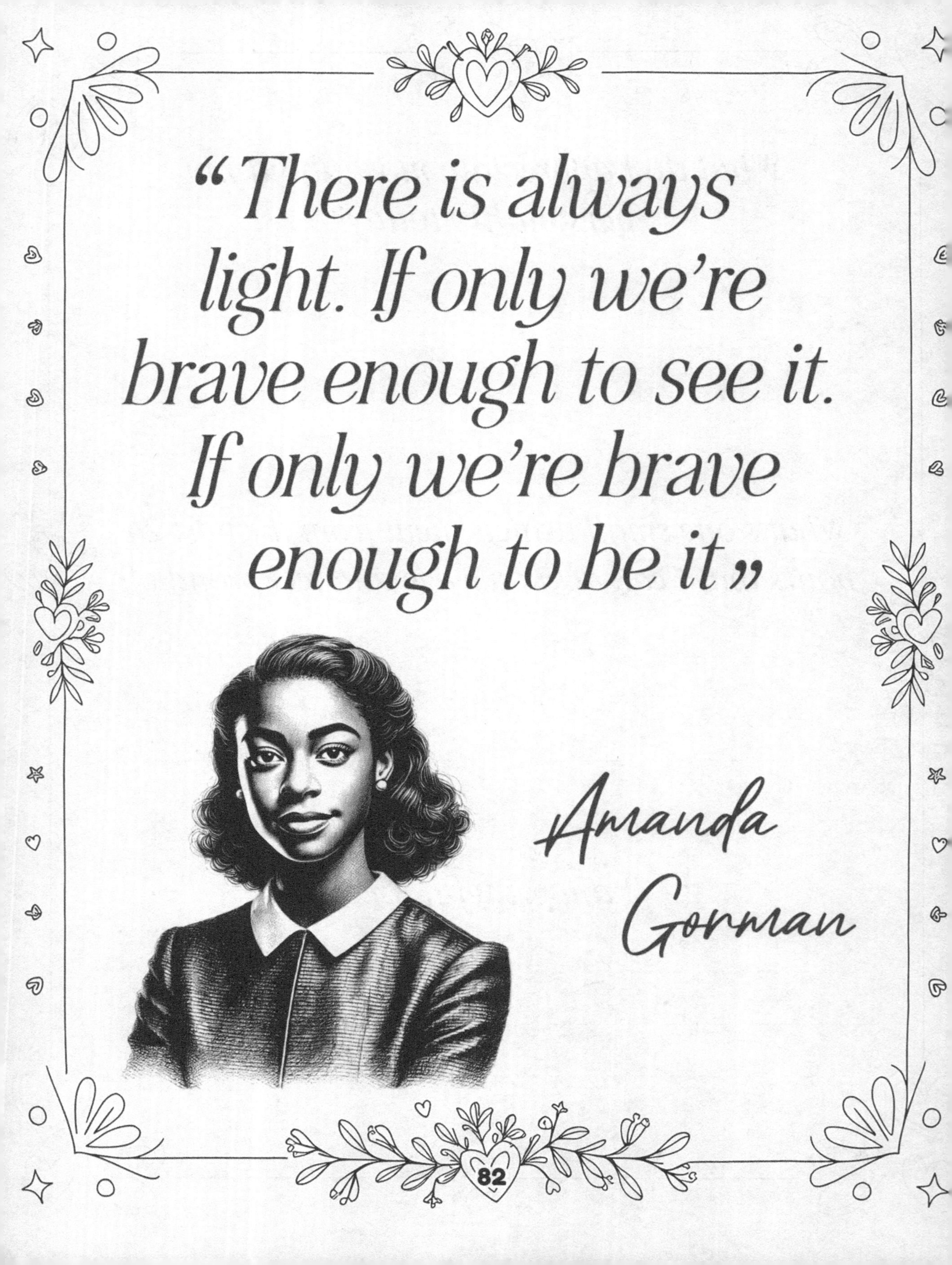
"There is always light. If only we're brave enough to see it. If only we're brave enough to be it"
Amanda Gorman
82

Day 27

What is one compliment I can give myself right now, without hesitation?

What negative thought about myself do I need to rewrite into something more loving or supportive?

I am grateful for...

1.

2.

3.

"Hard days are the best because that's when champions are made"
Gabby Douglas

Day
28

What is one small act of kindness I can do for myself today?

When I look in the mirror, what do I notice that is beautiful about me (inside or out)?

I am grateful for...

1.

2.

3.

What is my favorite inspirational quote or song lyric, and how does it uplift me?

Day
29

What do I appreciate most about my personality today?

What's one small achievement from the past 24 hours that I can acknowledge and feel proud of?

I am grateful for...

1.

2.

3.

“I am no longer accepting the things I cannot change. I am changing the things I cannot accept”

Angela Davis

Day 30

What is one compliment I can give myself right now, without hesitation?

What negative thought about myself do I need to rewrite into something more loving or supportive?

I am grateful for...

1.

2.

3.

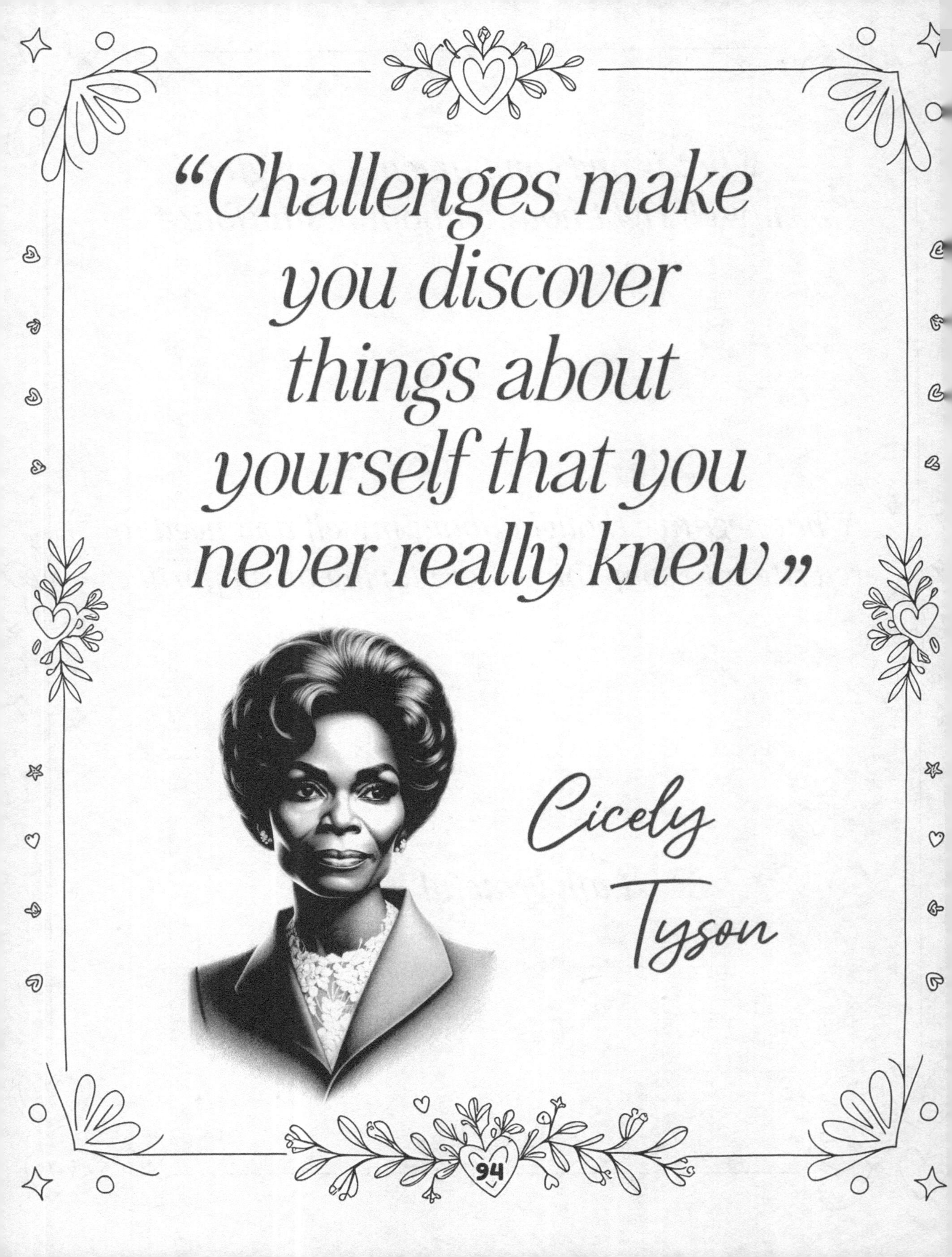
"Challenges make you discover things about yourself that you never really knew"
Cicely Tyson

Day
31

What is one small act of kindness I can do for myself today?

When I look in the mirror, what do I notice that is beautiful about me (inside or out)?

I am grateful for...

1.

2.

3.

What's something I used to struggle with that now feels easier, and how can I celebrate this progress?

Day 32

What do I appreciate most about my personality today?

What's one small achievement from the past 24 hours that I can acknowledge and feel proud of?

I am grateful for...

1.

2.

3.

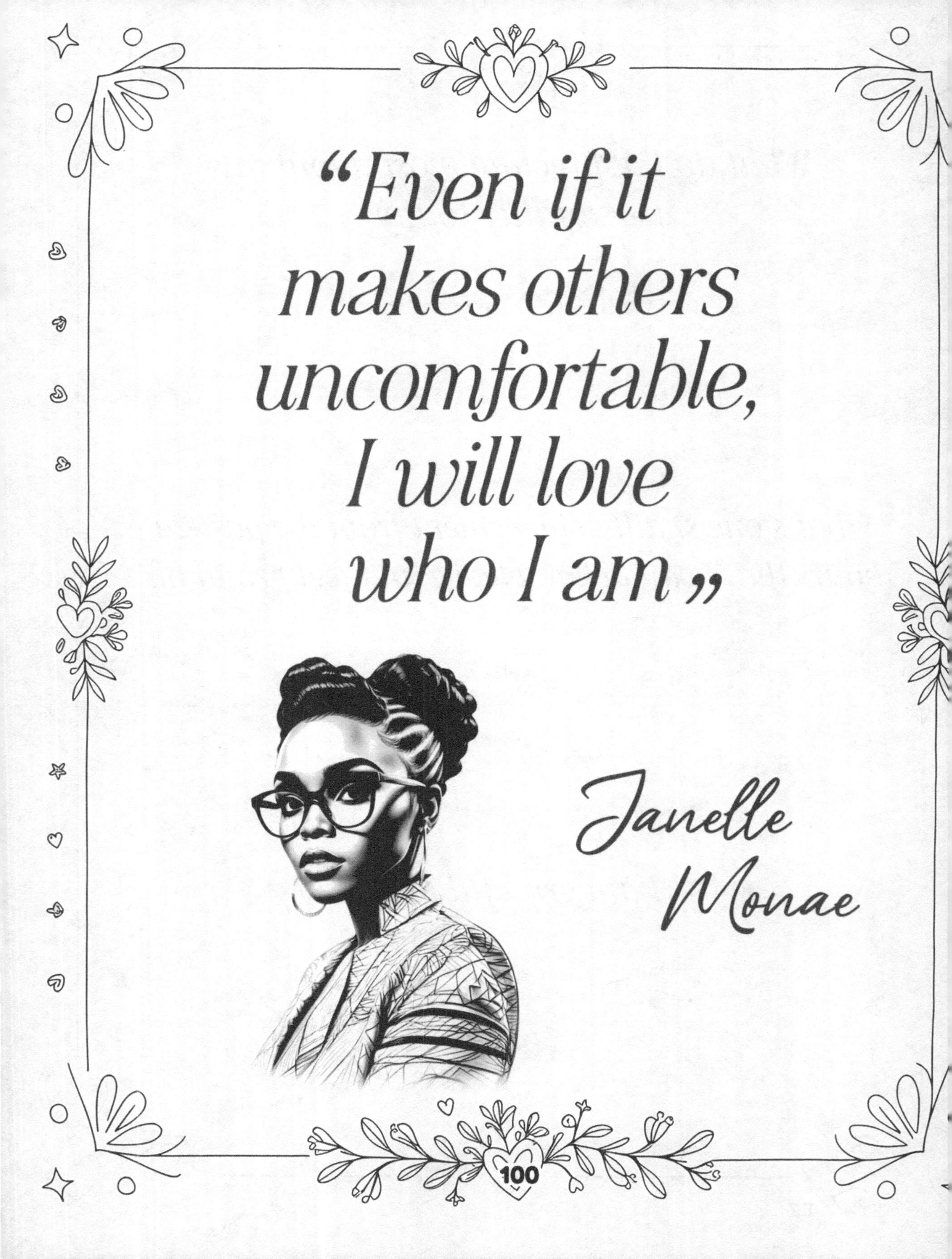
“Even if it makes others uncomfortable, I will love who I am”
Janelle Monae

Day
33

What is one compliment I can give myself right now, without hesitation?

What negative thought about myself do I need to rewrite into something more loving or supportive?

I am grateful for...

1.

2.

3.

"Each of us is on a journey of our own choosing.
I'm on my path, and you are on yours"
Laverne Cox

Made in United States
Cleveland, OH
21 May 2025